This book belongs to:

Portia
Polar Bear's
Birthday Wish

Story by Margie K. Carroll
Photography by Daniel J. Cox

Margie Carroll Press
Holly Springs, Georgia

Your mother is right.
You are perfect.

Portia

Hello, my name is Portia.

And this is my mom.

About one year ago . . .

I was a very lucky cub.

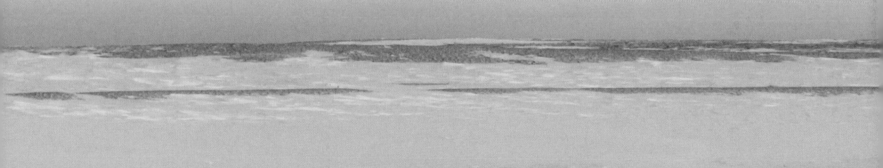

My home was beautiful with long days in the summer . . .

and long nights in the winter.

Many days were bright.

Some days were blue.

My life was perfect!

I learned to slide on my back . . .

and my stomach!

Yes, my life was perfect, until one spring day.

"Look Mom. There's Fiona Fox. May I go see her?"

"Yes, Dear, don't be long," Mom replied.

"Good morning, Fiona."

"Yes it is, Portia," Fiona replied.

"Oh, there is something I've been meaning to tell you.

Hmmm, how should I put this?

Well, I'll just say it.

Do you know you're pigeon-toed?"

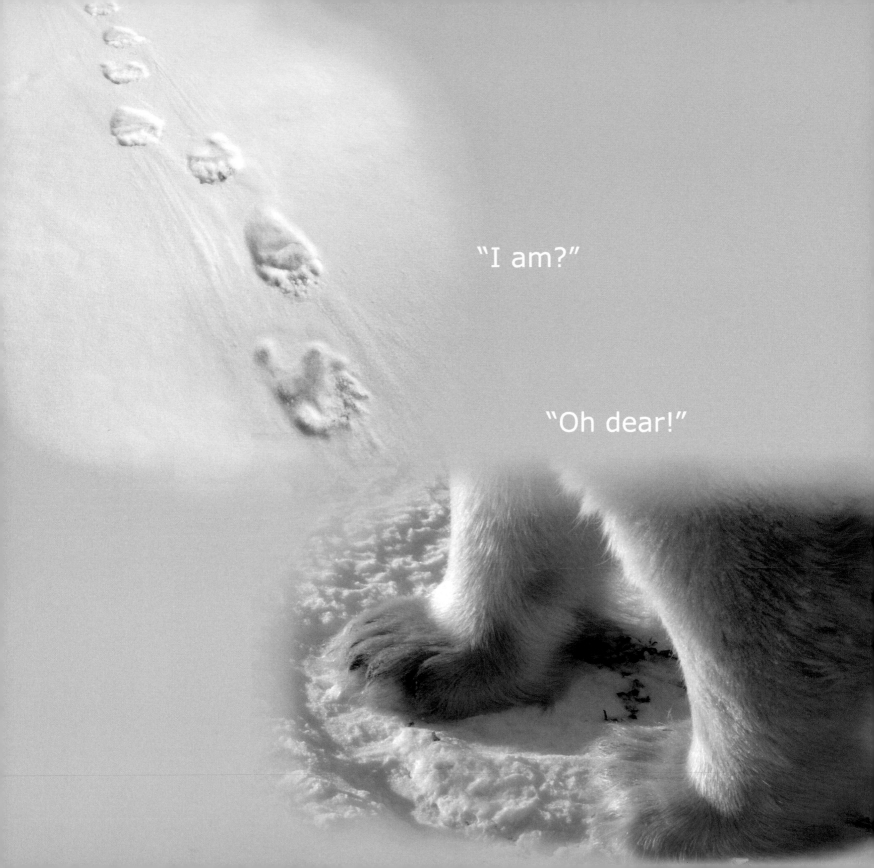

"Portia, come back. It's nap time."

"Good day, Harrison. May I ask you a question?"

"Certainly, Friend," he replied.

"Do you walk in a straight line?"

"No. But I hop in one," he added.

"Look, there are the Ptarmigan Travelers!"

"They walk straight, too . . .
when they are not walking in circles."

"I'm not normal, Mom."

"My dear Portia, you are perfect," Mom sighed.

But I could see Mom was worried, too.

Several months later I went to see Cesealia Seal.

"Good afternoon, Cesealia. I was wondering if you would show me your tracks?"

"Never mind."

It was time to visit Harrison again.
He would cheer me up.

"Oh, there you are, Harrison."

"Good afternoon, Portia. You seem worried," noticed Harrison.

"I am. I'm pigeon-toed, you know."

"Maybe this will help.
When you asked me before,
I'm afraid I wasn't totally
honest.   munch, munch

Yes, I do hop straight,
but my back feet land in
front of my front feet!

Fiona pointed that out
to me.   munch

I figure that makes me
tricky. Others can't tell
whether I am coming or
going!   munch

Besides, Portia, I like you
the way you are."

"Thank you, Harrison," I
replied.

That helped a little, but I was still pigeon-toed.

"Hi Leonard Lemming. Would you show me your tracks?"

"Okay. But don't follow me," he huffed.

Hmmmmm, too tiny to tell.

"Mom, I'm not normal. All my friends have straight legs: Fiona Fox, Harrison Hare, the Ptarmigan Travelers and probably Leonard Lemming and Cesealia Seal. Well, not Cesealia."

"Dear, you are absolutely perfect," said Mom.

"Portia, I'm pigeon-toed, too.
It runs in our family.

Being pigeon-toed helps us swim,
test the ice thickness . . .

and walk easily on
slippery snow."

"What nose?"

"There goes the Caribou Adventure Club," Mom noted.

"Oh, no! Straight tracks."

"Portia, tomorrow is your birthday. Do you have a special wish?" Mom asked.

"I just wish to be normal."

"Wake up, Portia. The Northern Lights
are wishing you a Happy Birthday!
And some visitors have passed. Do you
see their tracks?"

"Yes, I see them. They look like me and they are pigeon-toed, too! Maybe I AM normal after all!"

"Yes, Portia. You are perfectly normal. Happy Birthday!" whispered Mom.

Polar Bear Particulars

- The polar bear, *Ursus maritimus*, evolved from brown bear ancestors about 200,000 years ago. Also known as the sea bear, polar bears are well adapted for the harsh climate of the Far North.
- Five nations have polar bear populations: the United States (Alaska), Canada, Russia, Denmark (Greenland) and Norway. Polar bears range throughout the Arctic in areas where they hunt seals at openings in sea ice called leads. They are the top of the food chain in the Arctic and are the world's largest land predators.
- Ringed seals are their food of choice. Adult male polar bears weigh from 775 to more than 1,500 pounds. Females normally weigh 330 to 550 pounds.
- Females usually have two cubs, however; single cubs and triplets also occur. Cubs stay with their mom for up to 30 months.
- Polar bear's bodies are long and tapered. Their long necks are helpful when looking in holes for seals.
- Known for their incredible sense of smell, eyesight and hearing, the polar bear is well equipped to survive and even thrive in the harsh, arctic conditions.
- Polar bear paws measure up to 12 inches across and help distibute the weight when treading on thin ice. They act like huge paddles when swimming. Their feet have black footpads with small, soft bumps and tufts of fur between their toes (adapted for traction). Polar bear claws are curved and strong. They can measure more than two inches long.
- With their small ears and short tails, polar bears conserve heat.
- A polar bear's fur looks white, but it is not. Each hair shaft is transparent and pigment-free.
- Polar bears have black skin.
- A layer of thick blubber up to 4.5 inches thick helps insulate the bears from heat loss.
- In fact, polar bears can overheat when they run.

Portia Polar Bear had a wish and so do we.
Our wish is that you join with us and Polar Bears International (PBI) to help in its efforts to bring awareness and solutions to the plight of polar bears. Please check out its website: polarbearsinternational.org to see how we all can be a part of the solution to save the habitats of these magnificent creatures.
A portion of the proceeds from this book go to help PBI in its efforts.

Margie K. Carroll is a retired educator, Media Specialist, computer programmer and Technology Specialist. She enjoys writing, bicycling, traveling and wildlife photography.

Observing and photographing animal behavior is a fascinating second career. Margie's book series for children uses her photography and story-telling skills to illuminate an animal family's experiences from the point of view of their offspring.

Margie lives in Canton, Georgia, where she enjoys the company of deer, raccoons, rabbits, numerous song birds and several alert cats at her studio in the woods.

For nearly 30 years, Daniel J. Cox has been pursuing his life-long dream of photographing nature in all its elements. He has traveled to all seven continents in search of the images that inspire his art and inform his audience. Dan's work has been recognized and awarded in competitions including the BBC Wildlife Photographer of the Year and Nature's Best. He has been featured in galleries such as Nikon House, NY, the Natural History Museum in London and the National Museum of Wildlife Art in Jackson, Wyoming.

Dan is a regular contributor to natural history publications worldwide. He works with Hewlett Packard as a consultant for their fine art printers, has been honored as a "Nikon Legend" and is a mentor for American Photo's "Mentor Series" photography workshops.

His most personally satisfying accomplishments, however, include his two cover stories for *National Geographic Magazine* as well as his current volunteer work as a communications specialist and advisory council member for Polar Bears International. He is sole photographer for thirteen books including *Whitetail Country* that sold over 150,000 copies.

To learn more about Daniel visit www.naturalexposures.com

All photos are of wild and free roaming animals.

Special thanks to Esther, Pat, Doris, Val, Carol and Linda.

Printed in Hong Kong

info@naturalexposures.com

Margie K. Carroll
email: coalcat@mac.com
678-488-5183

Margie Carroll Press
P.O Box 581
Holly Springs, GA 30142